THIS BOOK BELONGS TO

____

SCHOOL YEAR ____________

Made in United States
North Haven, CT
16 June 2022

20320733R00062